FLORIST

MAKERS AND ARTISANS

JOSH GREGORY

Published in the United States of America by Cherry Lake Publishing Group
Ann Arbor, Michigan
www.cherrylakepublishing.com

Reading Adviser: Beth Walker Gambro, MS, Ed., Reading Consultant, Yorkville, IL
Photo Credits: © YAKOBCHUK VIACHESLAV/Shuttertstock.com, cover, 1, 24; © DimaBerlin/Shutterstock.com, 5; © Olena Yakobchuk/Shutterstock.com, 6; © industryviews/Shutterstock.com, 8; © Sladic/iStock.com, 9; © Rawpixel.com/Shutterstock.com, 10; © yangphoto/iStock.com, 13; © LightField Studios/Shutterstock.com, 14; © Geber86/iStock.com, 17, 18; © Fusionstudio/Shutterstock.com, 21; © Robert Kneschke/Shutterstock.com, 23; © Sina Ettmer Photography/Shutterstock.com, 27; © Nicholas Lamontanaro/Shutterstock.com, 28

Copyright © 2022 by Cherry Lake Publishing Group
All rights reserved. No part of this book may be reproduced or utilized in any form or by any means without written permission from the publisher.

Cherry Lake Press is an imprint of Cherry Lake Publishing Group.

Library of Congress Cataloging-in-Publication Data

Names: Gregory, Josh, author.
Title: Florist / by Josh Gregory.
Description: Ann Arbor, Michigan : Cherry Lake Publishing, [2022] | Series: Makers and artisans | Includes bibliographical references and index. | Audience: Grades 4-6
Identifiers: LCCN 2021007831 (print) | LCCN 2021007832 (ebook) | ISBN 9781534187276 (hardcover) | ISBN 9781534188679 (paperback) | ISBN 9781534190078 (pdf) | ISBN 9781534191471 (ebook)
Subjects: LCSH: Floristry—Vocational guidance—Juvenile literature. | Flower arrangement—Juvenile literature.
Classification: LCC SB449 .G683 2022 (print) | LCC SB449 (ebook) | DDC 745.92023—dc23
LC record available at https://lccn.loc.gov/2021007831
LC ebook record available at https://lccn.loc.gov/2021007832

Cherry Lake Publishing Group would like to acknowledge the work of the Partnership for 21st Century Learning, a Network of Battelle for Kids. Please visit http://www.battelleforkids.org/networks/p21 for more information.

Printed in the United States of America
Corporate Graphics

ABOUT THE AUTHOR

Josh Gregory is the author of more than 150 books for kids. He has written about everything from animals to technology to history. A graduate of the University of Missouri-Columbia, he currently lives in Chicago, Illinois.

TABLE OF CONTENTS

CHAPTER 1
Nature's Artwork 4

CHAPTER 2
In Full Bloom 12

CHAPTER 3
A Colorful Career 20

CHAPTER 4
Amazing Arrangements 26

CRAFT ACTIVITY 30

FIND OUT MORE 31

GLOSSARY 32

INDEX 32

CHAPTER 1

Nature's Artwork

Outside, the sky is gray. A damp, chilly breeze sends a shiver down your spine as you walk along the sidewalk. Winter has arrived, and the unpleasant weather makes you feel glum. But as you open the door of the floral shop and step inside, your mood is instantly lifted. All around you, bright colors burst from every direction. Flowers are carefully arranged in beautiful bundles. Delicate scents perfume the air. Leafy green plants hang from the ceiling in baskets, and potted trees stand tall in the corners. Behind the counter, an employee is placing flowers in a glass vase. Watching him work, you're amazed at the care he puts into each and every decision. You realize that the beautiful **bouquets** that fill the store were no accident. They are works of art created by talented people called florists.

Flowers and plants come in all shapes and sizes.

Flowers are an important part of special occasions such as weddings.

With their incredible variety of colors, **textures**, and shapes, flowers are naturally beautiful. All you need to do to enjoy them is take a walk outside. But as beautiful as flowers growing in the wild can be, a little human creativity can turn them into something completely different. People have been using flowers to decorate and make art since the earliest days of civilization. They can be grown in carefully managed gardens or pots of soil. They can be woven into wreaths and garlands, worn in the hair, or turned into a sort of living jewelry. They can be dried to preserve them as long-lasting decorations. And perhaps most interestingly of all, flowers can be cut from their plants and arranged in eye-catching combinations.

Greenhouses allow flowers to bloom year-round.

Flowers have been grown as crops for centuries. This practice really took off in the 1600s. That's when the earliest **greenhouses** were invented. They provide flowers with a warm environment year-round. Local growers delivered fresh flowers to floral shops and markets. Over time, growing technology improved beyond basic

[21ST CENTURY SKILLS LIBRARY]

Flowers in greenhouses still need to be cared for.

The art of caring for and arranging flowers is called floristry.

greenhouses, allowing growers to raise flowers from all around the world in almost any location. Refrigerated transport made it possible for plants to be transported long distances without spoiling. Today, you can walk into a flower shop and find a truly remarkable variety of plants, no matter where you live or what time of year it is.

While anyone can create their own flower arrangements at home, most people rely on professional florists when they want to add a little color to their environment. We use them to celebrate holidays such as Valentine's Day and Mother's Day. A bouquet of flowers can be a perfect gift to congratulate someone on a big achievement or let them know you're thinking of them during a tough time. And, of course, fresh flowers can also just brighten up a room.

Growing Something New

Earth has almost 400,000 different plant **species**, and almost all of them are able to produce some kind of flower. Thousands of previously unknown plants are discovered in the wild every year. But for some flower fanatics, even that isn't enough. Flower **breeding** is the centuries-old tradition of growing plants to emphasize certain **traits**. To do this, breeders carefully select which plants are allowed to reproduce and create new plants. Each new plant is likely to share the traits of its parents. Over the course of several plant generations, breeders can introduce new traits to different plant species or get rid of undesirable ones. Breeders have used this technique to create everything from larger versions of common flowers to brand-new color variations.

CHAPTER 2

In Full Bloom

Full-time florists are passionate about plants. For most of them, it's more than just a job. It's a way to express their creativity and enjoy the satisfaction of making other people happy.

Customer service is a huge part of working as a florist. Custom orders make up a lot of the average florist's business. This might be as simple as creating a bouquet for someone to give as a gift, or it could be a huge project like supplying all of the flowers for a wedding. Either way, the project will always begin with talking to a customer and finding out what they need. The customer might already have something in mind, or they might need help choosing.

Most shops offer premade arrangements that customers can buy.

Because flowers wilt so quickly, florists must time making their arrangements perfectly.

It's the florist's job to offer advice about what kinds of flowers will work best for the situation and fit the customer's budget.

The next step is for the florist to obtain the materials needed for the project. Some kinds of flowers and other decorations are likely kept in stock at all times. But if the florist is looking for something unique or needs a large quantity of flowers to fill an order, they might need to place special orders with their suppliers. Florists often buy their flowers from **wholesalers**. Sometimes, they work directly with local farmers. Flowers should be as fresh as possible. That means the florist needs to make sure everything is ready by the time the customer needs it, but not too far ahead of time. It requires careful planning and scheduling.

Florists put their creativity to work when actually assembling their arrangements. They don't simply place a bunch of flowers together at random. Each decision has an effect on the final result, so florists think carefully as they work. All the basic principles of art and design play a part in creating a beautiful flower arrangement. Color combinations are very important. Some colors work well with others, while some clash. Some colors are also more appropriate than others for certain occasions.

The florist also considers the size, shape, and texture of the flowers and positions them carefully. This might mean making sure different colors are distributed evenly or that some flowers aren't hidden behind others. It also means paying attention to the arrangement's overall shape. For example, some arrangements might be designed to be almost round, like a globe made of flowers. Others might be designed to hang down over the edges of a vase or stand tall. Flower arrangement options are unlimited. While there are plenty of well-known combinations that many customers will request, florists sometimes get to flex their creativity and try things that no one has ever seen before.

Daily Duties

Florists often do much more than create flower arrangements. In addition to answering phone calls and working the cash register, they might keep track of what they have in stock and what needs to be ordered. They also prepare freshly arrived flowers for sale, keep everything clean, and arrange things to look nice in the store. After all, presentation is everything when you are trying to sell things that look good!

Florists must also spend time each day doing basic shopkeeping tasks.

Each flower must be trimmed before it is placed in the arrangement. First, the florist must figure out how long the stem should be. Adjusting this will change the flower's height within the arrangement. Then, the florist cuts the end of the stem at an angle. This makes it easier for the stem to absorb water, which keeps the arrangement fresh longer. Any leaves along the stem are typically

Bendable wires can be used to hold flowers in place and keep the arrangement from moving around.

trimmed, though the florist might leave some near the top of the stem for visual effect. Lower leaves are always trimmed so they don't take up space or start to rot in the arrangement's water.

Many floral arrangements contain more than flowers. A florist might include blades of long grasses or twigs with bright berries attached. They might also add dried flowers or even artificial items made from plastic. Finally, the arrangement might be placed inside a vase or wrapped in plastic, ready for the customer to place inside their own vase. Adding fresh water to the vase helps the flowers stay alive even though they are no longer attached to living plants. The vase's appearance can also add to the overall effect.

For some projects, the florist might let the customer know that the arrangement is ready to be picked up. But most florists also offer delivery services. This comes in handy when a customer wants to have flowers sent to a friend or when large amounts of flowers are needed for an event. Arrangements must be carefully packed and loaded into refrigerated trucks. For larger deliveries, the florists might need to help unload and make sure the flowers get set up correctly.

CHAPTER 3

A Colorful Career

Being a florist isn't easy. There are always new arrangements to make and deadlines to meet. A good florist has to be friendly and hardworking. But if you like the idea of getting paid to work with flowers, it might be the right job for you.

Pretty much anyone can start down the path of becoming a florist. All you need are some flowers and something to hold them. If you have these things, you can make your own floral

A good florist must be creative.

arrangements at home. Visit your library for books about the principles of floral design or check online guides and video tutorials. You might also be able to find online or in-person classes if you want more personalized training.

In school, try to learn as much as you can about plants and how they grow. Biology, **horticulture**, and **agriculture** are all useful sciences for a florist to study. Art classes can help you develop a sense of style and learn how colors relate to each other. Business topics such as accounting and marketing will also come in handy, especially if you plan to open your own flower shop someday.

Season to Season

Florists tend to cycle through busy and slow seasons depending on the time of year. Around holidays like Valentine's Day, a florist might be so busy that they have to work extra hours. During the warm months of the year, many florists are busy with weddings. But there are also times when florists might go a few weeks without any major holidays or other events.

A job at a flower shop is a great first step at becoming a florist.

Some people attend college before beginning careers as florists. An associate's or bachelor's degree in horticulture or art can offer skills and knowledge that will help you become a better florist. However, finding work in the floral business generally doesn't require a degree. Many people begin their careers with a job as an assistant or cashier at a flower shop. These jobs generally don't have many requirements. You might even be able to get one before

Most florists work at small shops or run their own shops.

finishing high school. Working at a flower shop, you'll get to see firsthand how everything works. And if you express an interest in learning more, the more experienced florists at the shop might be willing to teach you. This is perhaps the best way to learn the ins and outs of the business.

As you get more experience in the field, you may find other job opportunities. For example, you might work helping people decorate their homes or plan events. Or if you have a special knack for raising plants, you might try working at a greenhouse or flower farm. Flowers are a big industry, and there are a lot of options.

CHAPTER 4

Amazing Arrangements

Even the simplest floral arrangement is usually enough to brighten a room. But some florists like to work on projects that are anything but simple. For example, can you imagine exploring a life-size castle of flowers? In 2019, workers at a park in Chengdu, China, assembled a structure that was more than 123 feet (37 meters) long, 85 feet (26 m) wide, and 76 feet (23 m) tall, covered entirely in live flowers. After building the main shape of the castle from steel, they arranged more than 74,000 plants to create the colorful exterior. And that's not even the tallest flower arrangement ever made. In 2013, an arrangement standing more than 89 feet (27 m) was assembled in Mexico City, Mexico, as part of a Mother's Day celebration. This record has yet to be topped.

Flower sculptures can be arranged into any shape.

Flower arrangements don't have to be big to be amazing, though. Next time your family hosts a holiday gathering, ask if you can make a centerpiece for the table. It could help make the gathering special. Or simply try putting some flowers in your room. You might be surprised at how much nicer it is to start your day by looking at a lively, colorful arrangement.

Be sure to take time to notice the flowers you see in everyday life. What kinds stand out to you? What makes some arrangements

An Earth goddess sculpture in Atlanta, Georgia.

more appealing than others? The more you look at flowers and consider them carefully, the more you'll develop your own tastes and sense of style. Examining other things can also give you ideas for flower arrangements. For example, the colors in a painting might inspire a unique combination of flowers. A tree's shape might give you an idea for how to position flowers. You never know where inspiration will come from, so keep your eyes open wherever you go. Before you know it, you'll be a flower-arranging pro!

Around the World

Many cultures have their own unique flower-arranging traditions. Some have lasted for centuries or even longer. For example, Japan has a rich history of flower arranging. Many of the country's floral traditions have their roots in Buddhist religious teachings. Flowers might be arranged to **symbolize** various aspects of nature.

Today, many florists take inspiration from these kinds of global cultural traditions. It's not uncommon to find American florists who have studied the history of French or Chinese floral arranging. By combining these traditions with the latest techniques and the wider variety of flowers available today, florists can always create something unique.

Craft Activity

Make Your Own Floral Arrangement

Want to try arranging flowers for yourself? It's easy, and you don't need many things to get started. Just buy some assorted fresh flowers from a local florist or grocery store and jump right in.

SUPPLIES

- A variety of flowers
- Water
- Scissors
- Vase

STEPS

1. Take a look at the flowers you have to work with, as well as the size and shape of your vase. Before you do anything, decide what kind of shape you want your arrangement to have. Where should different flowers be placed?

2. Carefully place flowers in the vase, one by one. Trim each flower with the scissors before adding it. Remove most of the leaves. Then, cut the end of the stem at an angle. The length of the stem will determine how high the flower sticks up out of the vase.

3. Feel free to move things and rearrange as you work. You probably won't get everything exactly right on the first try. That's okay! It's all about making sure the final product looks nice.

4. Once you're satisfied, add some water to the vase. Use room-temperature or slightly warm water, and fill the vase about two-thirds to three-fourths full. Be sure to change the water every few days to make your flowers last longer.

5. Set the vase somewhere where it will fit in with the surroundings. Congratulations! You're officially a floral arranger.

Find Out More

BOOKS

Crary, Calvert. *Flower School: A Practical Guide to the Art of Flower Arranging.* New York, NY: Black Dog and Leventhal, 2020.

McLaughlin, Suzi. *The Paper Florist.* London, England: Kyle Books, 2019.

WEBSITES

U.S. Bureau of Labor Statistics Occupational Outlook Handbook— Floral Designers
www.bls.gov/ooh/arts-and-design/floral-designers.htm
Check out official data about employment rates, average salaries, and more for floral designers.

YouTube—The Elements and Principles of Floral Design
www.youtube.com/watch?v=b-L8_LSRj_4
Learn the basic ideas behind creating appealing floral arrangements with this short video.

GLOSSARY

agriculture (AG-ruh-kuhl-chur) the science of farming

bouquets (boh-KAYS) arranged bundles of flowers

breeding (BREE-ding) the controlled reproduction of animals and plants

greenhouses (GREEN-houss-ehs) buildings that trap energy from sunlight to keep plants warm in cold weather

horticulture (HOR-tuh-kuhl-chur) the science of growing plants

species (SPEE-sheez) a grouping of living things that are able to mate and produce offspring together

symbolize (SIM-buh-lize) to stand for or represent something else

textures (TEKS-churz) the feel and appearance of an object's surface

traits (TRATES) qualities or characteristics that make something different from others

wholesalers (HOHL-say-luhrz) businesses that buy goods from producers in large quantities to resell to stores

INDEX

arrangements/arranging,
    floral craft activity, 30
    developing personal style, 29
    examples of projects, 26–29
    other materials in, 18–19
    premade, 13
    records, 26
art, 7
art and design principles, 15–16
Atlanta, Georgia, 28

bouquets, 4, 11, 12, 13
breeding, 11

centerpieces, 27
Chengdu, China, 26
color combinations, 15
craft activity, 30
creativity, 7, 12, 15, 21
customer service, 12, 14

decorating, 7
delivery service, 19

farmers, 15

florist
    as a career, 20–25
    creativity, 12, 15, 21
    daily duties, 16, 17
    developing personal style, 29
    education, 22–23
    inspiration, 29
    introduction to, 4–11
    job opportunities, 25
    obtaining materials, 14–15
    seasonal cycles, 22
    skills and assets, 21
    ways to become one, 23, 25
    what the job is, 12–19
floristry, 10
flower shop, 4, 23–25
flowers, 4, 5, 6
    arranging.
        See arrangements/
        arranging, floral.
    breeding, 11
    craft activity, 30
    and decorating, 7
    examples of projects, 26–29
    freshness, 15
    as inspiration, 29
    sculptures, 27, 28
    uses for, 11

greenhouses, 8, 9

holidays, 11, 22

inspiration, 29

Japan, 29

leaves, 17–18

Mexico City, Mexico, 26

orders, custom, 12

plants, 4, 5, 11, 12

sculptures, 27, 28
special occasions, 6, 11, 12, 22
stems, 17–18

technology, growing, 8, 10
traditions, cultural, 29
traits, 11
transportation, refrigerated, 10

vases, 19

weddings, 6, 12, 22
wholesalers, 15